The
BANNED BOOK
of MARY

Presented to Purchase College
by
Gary Waller, PhD Cambridge

State University of New York
Distinguished Professor

Provost 1995-2004
Professor of Literature & Cultural Studies
Professor of Theatre & Performance
1995-2019

The
BANNED BOOK
of MARY

How Her Story Was
Suppressed by the
Church and Hidden in
Art for Centuries

❀ RONALD F. HOCK ❀

Ulysses Press

Contents

INTRODUCTION

In Cologny, a pastoral lakeside village on the outskirts of Geneva, Switzerland, stands the Bodmer Library and Museum, a favorite haunt of scholars and tourists alike. As you stand in its hushed, lofty central atrium, you find yourself surrounded by two-story-high tiers of shelves containing one of the world's finest private collections of rare books and documents—more than 160,000 in all. You can sense the power of the written word radiating from illuminated medieval manuscripts, a first-edition Gutenberg Bible, handwritten texts of Homer's *Odyssey,* Dante's *Divine Comedy,* Chaucer's *Canterbury Tales,* and Grimm's *Fairy Tales,* and first editions of Cervantes's *Don Quixote* and Shakespeare's

Comedies, essays by Sir Isaac Newton, and the notebooks of Albert Einstein.

Among the most remarkable of the library's holdings are twenty-two ancient Christian manuscripts known as the Bodmer Papyri. The library's founder, the late Martin Bodmer, discovered them during the 1950s—not in an archaeological dig, but among the antiquities dealers who inhabit the shadowy world where such objects find their way from the hands of looters and tomb raiders to the curators of the world's great museums.

Experts believe that most of the Bodmer Papyri came from a small library maintained by monks at Faw Qibli, said to be the world's oldest Christian monastery, near the Egyptian city of Dishna. The keepers of sacred books sealed them in jars and hid them. Perhaps, as most present-day experts say, they had to save these secret papers from Arab invaders. Or, as some modern scholars speculate, the idea may have been to give worn documents a decent burial after new copies had been made. Preserved by the bone-dry desert climate, the papyri lay concealed for some 1500 years before local peasants unearthed them in the mid-twentieth century.

As a sightseer, you can only see photocopies of sections of these papyri. If you can persuade the library administrators that you have a compelling reason to examine the originals, you will find them in a climate-controlled room under the watchful eyes of Swiss security guards.

Among the Bodmer Library's papyri is the oldest known copy of the Gospel of Luke, dating to around 200 AD, and one of the Gospel of the John, also from around 200. Among these papyri are also copies of the Letters of James, Peter, John, and Jude.

The most enigmatic document in the collection, known as Bodmer Papyrus V, is not part of the biblical canon, though perhaps it should have been. It bears the title *The Birth of Mary, Revelation of James.* It is the oldest known copy, and one of the most complete, of a book referred to by modern scholars as the *Protevangelium Jacobi* or, translated into English, the *Infancy Gospel of James.*

Like all papyri, this one was made from a type of reed that the Egyptians cultivated along the banks of the Nile River. Skilled artisans would slice the pith of the reed in long, wafer-thin strips, which they would lay vertically side-by-side on a damp surface. Then they would lay another layer of strips horizontally across the first and pound them with a hammer until they adhered together. Polished with pumice, sheets or scrolls of papyrus made writing paper that was prized throughout the ancient world for its durability, and a remarkable number of papyrus documents have survived to the present era.

Leonardo da Vinci (1452-1519)
The Virgin and Child with Saint Anne, Louvre, Paris

Saint Anne, Mary's mother, appears nowhere in the Bible. Yet she was easily recognizable to Leonardo da Vinci and his contemporaries because they were familiar with the stories of Mary's life that originated in the second-century Infancy Gospel of James.

Not surprisingly, Bodmer Papyrus V is frayed along the edges. Its originally white surface has darkened to a cinnamon color, and the ink, made from lampblack dissolved in papyrus juice, has faded with age. The writing surface is covered almost edge-to-edge with Greek capital letters, written—as was the custom of the time—without spaces between words.

This document is the source of almost all the details we believe we know about the life of Mary, the mother of Jesus Christ. It also sets forth an account of the birth of Jesus that is much different from the Christmas story accepted around the world today. Written around 150 AD by an unknown Christian, it was widely known in many parts of the early Christian world; yet few people today have ever heard of it.

THE LEGEND OF MARY

While the New Testament focuses on Mary and Joseph in the context of the birth of Jesus, the Infancy Gospel of James begins years earlier by describing the plight of an elderly couple named Joachim and Anne. Though prosperous and prominent, they are childless, a condition not acceptable to the society of their time. In fact, Joachim alone of all the good people in Israel has no children.

Giotto di Bondone (1266-1336)
The Dream of Joachim, Scrovegni Chapel, Padua

In a series of frescoes, the Renaissance master Giotto di Bondone
illustrated episodes from the life of Mary—all drawn from later
adaptations of the banned Infancy Gospel of James. Here, a messenger
of God tells Mary's father Joachim that his wife will bear a child.

After Joachim is publicly chastised for his lack of
offspring and his offerings to God are rejected by the
priests, he decides to retreat into the wilderness to fast
and pray in the hope that God will tell him why he is
childless. His wife Anne is similarly blamed by her own

slave for being barren. Stricken with sorrow, she sits in her garden only to be further reminded of her barrenness by the fruitfulness of everything around her.

An angel hears Anne's lament and informs her that she will bear a child who will be known throughout the world. In the desert, Joachim is likewise told that his prayers have been heard. Overcome with joy, Anne vows to dedicate her child to God, and Joachim rushes from the desert to be reunited with his wife. The child, of course, is Mary.

After Mary's birth, Anne transforms the baby's bedroom into a sanctuary where nothing unclean can touch her. On the young girl's first birthday, the priests bless her. Then when she is three, her parents fulfill their vow by presenting Mary to the priests in the Temple in Jerusalem. There she spends the rest of her childhood, fed by the hand of an angel.

None of this appears in the New Testament. Even when the Infancy Gospel begins to overlap with material in the gospels of Matthew and Luke (the only books of the Bible that describe the circumstances surrounding Jesus' birth), it tells a very different and much more detailed story. At the age of twelve, Mary is about to become a woman and hence a threat to the Temple's purity. Having sought divine guidance, the high priest is instructed to summon all the widowers of Israel. Each is to bring his staff. A sign will determine which of the suitors is to receive her as his wife.

Among the widowers is Joseph, who in this account is described as an old man with grown sons. A dove appears from the tip of Joseph's staff and perches on his head, indicating that he is the one chosen as Mary's husband. Joseph protests that he is elderly, with grown children, and does not wish to remarry. He relents only when the priests agree to let him take Mary as his ward, not his wife. Joseph takes Mary home, but soon his job as a carpenter calls for him to go out of town to build houses.

Together with other virgins, Mary is asked by the high priest to spin thread for a new temple veil. While drawing water from a well, Mary hears a voice. Terrified, she hurries home to her spinning. There the voice—that of an angel—addresses her again, saying that she has found favor with God and will conceive by means of His word. In a scene very similar to the Annunciation in the New Testament, she is told that the child will be divine and that she is to call him Jesus.

Mary finishes her spinning, takes her thread to the high priest, then goes to stay with her relative Elizabeth, who is herself pregnant with the child who will become John the Baptist. The details of their meeting are similar to those in the Gospel of Luke, complete with their greetings to one another and an incident in which the unborn John leaps for joy in his mother's womb.

Mary returns to Joseph's house after three months. After three more months, Joseph rejoins her there. Once again the story begins to diverge from the biblical account, adding biographical anecdotes that would inspire devotional artworks but never become part of the New Testament.

On finding Mary pregnant, Joseph initially blames himself for failing to protect her. Then he rebukes Mary sharply and, despite her claims of innocence, resolves to divorce her. But that night, Joseph has a dream in which an angel tells him that Mary is pregnant by the Holy Spirit and that he is to name the child Jesus. Obedient to the angel's message, Joseph abandons his thoughts of divorce.

A major crisis soon develops when a visitor realizes that Mary is pregnant and tells the high priest that Joseph has violated the virgin in his care. Summoning Joseph and Mary to answer this charge, the priest hears their denials. In a dramatic confrontation unknown to the New Testament, the priest refuses to believe them and orders Joseph to return Mary to the Temple. Joseph weeps at the thought of losing her, and the high priest partially relents by sending them into the wilderness to test their honesty. When they return unharmed, the priest realizes that they are innocent and publicly exonerates the couple.

From this point, James is similar in some respects to the birth stories in Matthew and Luke, but a close reading reveals many significant departures from the canonical accounts. Joseph and Mary heed Emperor Augustus' call for a census and head for Bethlehem, as in the Lukan account. But the author of the Infancy Gospel expands the narrative considerably. He adds a speech by Joseph detailing how Mary should be described for the census. There's a conversation between Joseph and Mary while they travel. Most importantly, they stop before reaching Bethlehem so that Mary can deliver her child—not in a stable but in a cave. Also included is a miraculous vision that Joseph experiences at the moment of Jesus' birth in which time stands still. Clouds and birds are frozen in the air, and men and animals remain motionless on the ground.

Where Luke tells of shepherds arriving from their fields, the Infancy Gospel has two midwives who visit the cave where Mary has given birth. Skeptical of the claim of one midwife that a virgin has given birth, the second midwife performs a physical examination to confirm that the child has indeed been born to a virgin. But as she touches Mary, her hand begins to burn, and she prays for help. A voice tells her to pick up the baby Jesus. When she does, her hand is healed.

As Joseph, Mary, and the infant Jesus are preparing to leave for Bethlehem, the Magi arrive at the cave in search of the newborn king of the Judeans. Here, the Infancy Gospel's guiding star and the gifts of gold, frankincense, and myrrh recall the Gospel of Matthew. The Magi, as it turns out, have already informed King Herod of their search for one who has been born king of the Jews (a title held by Herod), though they have offered no clue to his whereabouts. As in the Bible, Herod's fear and rage lead him to order the murder of all male children under age two to insure the removal of his royal rival.

Then the Infancy Gospel departs once again from the traditional story. Instead of having Jesus escape Herod's soldiers by means of Joseph leading him and Mary into Egypt, his life is saved by Mary's courage as she wraps him in swaddling cloths and hides him in a manger in Bethlehem.

In a plot twist that may baffle modern readers, the Infancy Gospel drops the story of Mary, Joseph, and Jesus at this point, and the closing scene deals with the parents of John the Baptist, who is also among the infants endangered by Herod's murderous decree. Terrified, John's mother, Elizabeth, flees to the hills with her baby. John's father, Zechariah, who is serving at the time as a priest in the Temple, refuses to tell Herod's agents where his wife and child have gone. He pays for his silence with his life.

The Infancy Gospel of James ends with a simple prayer: "Grace will be with all those who fear the Lord. Amen."

The reason for the gospel's unusual structure, including the switch of characters in the final pages, is that it followed a formal literary style called an *encomium*, which—along with more familiar formats such as fables, mythological tales, and essays—was taught in school courses on composition throughout the Greco-Roman world. The encomium form, according to textbooks of the time, should end by comparing the subject's virtue, in this case, Mary's courage in saving the infant Jesus from Herod's assassins, with that of another well-known personage, namely the priest Zechariah's courage in protecting his own son from the same danger.

Recognizing the Infancy Gospel of James as an encomium tells us one important fact. This literary form was reserved especially for praising noteworthy people and was typically intended to be read aloud in public. As a book of praise, it would have been composed for celebratory occasions.

This one was most likely intended to be read during Christian worship and perhaps during a feast day.

Giotto di Bondone (1266-1336)
The Birth of Mary, Scrovegni Chapel, Padua
*Since the Bible says nothing of Mary's parentage and birth,
Giotto based this fresco on later adaptations of the banned
Infancy Gospel of James.*

Since no feast dedicated to Mary is known to have been observed by Christians as early as 150 AD, I believe it might have been written for the communion of the Lord's Supper. If so, the author had taken the commemoration of Christ's death to compose and deliver an encomium praising his mother, Mary. Later, Mary came to be celebrated in feast days of her own—the Feast of the Birth of Mary (September 8) and the Feast of the Presentation in the Temple (November 21). We know that the Infancy Gospel of James was traditionally read on those days since scribes who copied the gospel often wrote the dates September 8 or November 21 on the manuscripts.

THE FORGOTTEN BOOK OF MARY

Virtually all modern Christians accept without question the contents of the New Testament as they have been passed down through the centuries. But in the first centuries of the Christian era, the content of the Bible was not so clearly defined.

By the end of the second century, a generation or two after the Infancy Gospel of James was written, church scholars such as Bishop Irenaeus of Lyons and the Carthaginian priest Tertullian had defined which documents were indisputably authoritative, including the gospels of Matthew, Mark, Luke, and John as well as sixteen of the twenty-three other documents that make up the New Testament today. Many other writings were considered to be scriptural in some parts of the Christian world, and there was no general agreement about which of these works were *not* part of the Bible.

Among these writings was the Infancy Gospel of James. This account of Mary's ancestry and her life up to the time of Jesus' birth was popular among Ebionite

(Jewish) Christians as well as in Greek, Syrian, Coptic, and Armenian churches.

The gospel purports to have been written by a James, presumably James the brother of Jesus, shortly after 4 BC, when King Herod died. If true, this would place the Infancy Gospel among the earliest of all Christian writings, predating the crucifixion of Jesus by more than thirty years. The last chapter says, "Now I, James, am the one who wrote this account at the time when an uproar arose in Jerusalem at the death of Herod. I took myself to the wilderness until the uproar had died down." (See page 110.) Since it identifies James as one of Joseph's sons from a previous marriage, it suggests that the author was an eyewitness to many of the events it describes.

Modern scholars, using the methods of historical criticism, agree that James could not have been the real author of the Infancy Gospel. It contains elements that would only make sense to readers who were already familiar with the gospels of Matthew and Luke, which were written between 80 and 90 AD—at least twenty years after James died. In fact, a primary purpose of the Infancy Gospel was to answer questions about Jesus' parentage that were not addressed by Matthew or Luke. The real author wrote in the guise of James to enhance the Infancy Gospel's credibility.

The true authorship of the Infancy Gospel of James remains a mystery. All we know is that it was composed in the Greek region of the Roman Empire, sometime around 150 AD, by someone with a standard education but no exceptional writing talent; its grace and beauty come from its subject matter, not its author's eloquence. Although some clergymen today dismiss the Infancy Gospel as a "forgery," its authorship was unquestioned in earlier times and does nothing to explain why it was ultimately banned.

That the Infancy Gospel of James was widely accepted is clear from the fact that it was translated from the original Greek into at least eight other languages including Ethiopian, Arabic, and Irish. Strangely, though, after Latin became the official language of the church, it was not translated into that language for more than 500 years.

THE FORBIDDEN GOSPEL

To find out why the Infancy Gospel of James was excluded from the Bible and banned by the church, the best place to start is the library of Damasus I, who served as Pope from 366 AD until his death in 384. Pope Damasus built the first permanent structure to house the fast-growing collection of church archives, the forerunner of today's Vatican Library. He entrusted the archives to his secretary, Eusebius Sophronius Hieronymus, known today as Saint Jerome, the patron saint of librarians and translators.

It was Jerome who created the Latin Vulgate Bible, the definitive version of the scriptures used by the Roman Catholic Church to the present day, by revising, unifying, and translating both the Old and New Testaments into the Latin idiom spoken by residents of Rome at the time. The Pope gave him this assignment in 382 AD, following the convocation of the Council of Rome, over which Damasus presided. As a result of that meeting, the Pope issued a decree naming the books that would form the canon, or official contents, of the Bible. Damasus' list included several writings that had not previously been accepted as scriptural, but the Infancy Gospel of James was not among them.

It is easy to imagine Jerome at his work. He was a favorite subject of Renaissance painters. An oil painting done in 1521 by Albrecht Dürer, for instance, depicts the librarian as an old man with a long, wavy beard and a taciturn expression, running his left hand over a human skull symbolizing the brevity of life as he pores over a document on the desk in front of him.

It would have been obvious to Jerome that the thematic core of the Infancy Gospel of James was Mary's purity. Conceived through divine intervention and not lust, born to wealthy and pious parents, raised in a room as pure as a temple and then in the Temple itself, fed by angels, given to an old man who had no interest in her and who was out of town when the child was conceived, publicly exonerated by the high priest, and certified by midwives as virginal even after childbirth, Mary was the purest possible person God could have found to bear the Christ child.

Many artworks, such as one Leonardo da Vinci painted in 1480, depict Jerome with a lion at his side—a reference to the time he spent as a hermit in the desert. According to legend, he pulled a thorn from the lion's paw, and the lion remained his loyal companion for many years. If the story was factual, the lion must have been one of Jerome's few friends. Before becoming a priest, Jerome had been a lawyer, and as one of the most influential writers of his time he loved nothing more than arguing his own views in debates with other theologians—forcefully and sarcastically, often making vicious personal attacks against his adversaries.

Thus, about a year after he was first assigned to translate the holy scriptures, Jerome penned a treatise called "On the Perpetual Virginity of the Blessed Virgin." It was a response to an earlier tractate by a fellow priest named Helvidius who questioned whether Mary had remained ever-virginal after Jesus' birth. Helvidius

Giotto di Bondone (1266-1336)
The Marriage of the Virgin, Scrovegni Chapel, Padua

*The stories in the Infancy Gospel of James were adapted over
the centuries. The Infancy Gospel tells that Joseph refused to
marry Mary and instead took her as his ward. But an actual
marriage, illustrated here, occurs in the ninth-century
Book of the Birth of Mary.*

pointed to the brothers and sisters of Jesus named in
Mark 6:3 and Matthew 13:55 as proof that Mary and
Joseph had had a normal marriage. He backed up this
interpretation by quoting Luke 2:7, "Mary gave birth to
her first-born son" (suggesting that other children were
born to her later) and Matthew 1:25, "Joseph did not

know Mary until she had given birth to a son" (implying that the couple did have marital relations after Jesus' birth). For Helvidius, the marriage of Mary and Joseph showed that married women were just as glorious in the eyes of God as virgins—a view with which Jerome vehemently disagreed.

Jerome could easily have cited the Infancy Gospel of James as authority to support his argument. Though it was not one of the documents chosen by Pope Damasus to be in the Latin Vulgate Bible, it could have been asserted as a non-canonical authority, as writings by many early Christian theologians were. It was the first gospel to proclaim Mary's virginity after the birth of Jesus. Joseph's advanced age and his decision to be Mary's legal guardian rather than her husband, as well as the findings of the midwives that Mary was still intact after Jesus' birth, would certainly have bolstered Jerome's case for perpetual virginity. And yet . . .

Jerome did not use the Infancy Gospel as evidence because a single, seemingly insignificant detail called its accuracy into question, at least in his mind. He rejected the presence of the midwife who exclaimed that Mary was a virgin. Jerome saw this passage as flying in the face of Luke 2:7, which says that Mary wrapped Jesus in swaddling cloths. Since this was a task normally performed by a midwife, not the mother, no midwife could have been present at the nativity.

Instead, in his debate with Helvidius, Jerome fell back on his expertise as a translator, asserting that the words "brothers and sisters" did not always mean siblings by birth but were also used in a number of biblical passages to indicate brothers by race, kinship, or affection. When Matthew and Luke spoke of Jesus' "brothers and sisters," Jerome insisted, they meant "cousins." Thus, the words did not impugn Mary's perpetual virginity. Since Jerome was one of the most influential writers of his time, Helvidius' position was refuted and revealed as a heresy— and the Infancy Gospel of James was pushed aside.

This rejection was the first step toward banning the Infancy Gospel. The Council of Rome, where Pope Damasus handed down his original decree omitting the Infancy Gospel from the Bible, was local in scope—not an ecumenical council—so it was disregarded in other parts of the empire. Its decisions generally reflected Pope Damasus' personal views, which outside Rome were considered far from infallible. Elsewhere, the Infancy Gospel was still accepted by many as carrying significant authority.

Official and explicit rejection of the Infancy Gospel of James as apocryphal (rejected by the Church) would have to wait another century. In 496 AD, Pope Gelasius I handed down a decree, known as the *Decretum Galasianum*. The decree began by confirming the list of books Damasus I and Jerome had selected to make up the official biblical canon, but now added a long list of writings to be rejected, including about two dozen gospels, acts, letters, and revelations.

These writings, Gelasius said, had been "recognized by heretics or schismatics" and were to be avoided by Catholics. Among the banned writings, many of which are no longer known to exist in any form, was the Infancy Gospel of James, identified here as the Gospel under the name of James the Younger.

Not one to mince words, Gelasius proclaimed, "We acknowledge (these writings) to be not merely rejected but eliminated from the whole Roman Catholic and Apostolic Church and, with their authors and the followers of their authors, to be damned in the inextricable shackles of anathema forever."

With this decree, the book of Mary was banned— officially, at least. But it was too late.

THE RISE OF MARY

Even as church fathers were stripping the Infancy Gospel of James of its authority and ultimately condemning it as a heretical work to be wiped from the face of the earth, societal trends and historical events in other parts of the empire were exalting the importance of Mary and her perpetual chastity.

Although chastity emerged as a principal value in the Roman Empire by the time of the emergence of Christianity, the suffering caused by persecution and plague made martyrdom the ultimate virtue. Paul, the author of much of the New Testament, never mentioned the virginity of Jesus' mother, nor did Mark or John. The accounts of the immaculate conception and virgin birth in the gospels of Matthew and Luke may have been included less from any great regard for chastity than to show that Christ was the fulfillment of the Old Testament prophecy of Isaiah 7:14, "Behold, a virgin shall conceive, and bear a son, and shall call his name Immanuel [meaning "God is with us]." Matthew himself said as much (Matthew 1:23).

But by the time the Infancy Gospel of James was written, self-control or purity—a Greek ideal since the time of Socrates—was already becoming recognized by Christians as a highly valued human attainment. This virtue included control of the tongue, the belly, and, as the Greeks put it, "the things below the belly." Purity was glorified in second-century Greek philosophical treatises, rhetorical speeches, pastoral poems, satires, and epics written around the same time as the Infancy Gospel of James.

As the persecution of Christians ended with the reign of Emperor Constantine I in the early fourth century, purity came to replace martyrdom as the paramount Christian virtue. Mary's virginity, as expressed in the Infancy Gospel of James, made her the ultimate embodiment of purity. The immaculate conception and birth of Jesus began to take its place alongside His teachings, crucifixion, and resurrection as events important to Christian worship. This was reflected not only in Jerome's writings supporting the perpetual virginity of Mary but also in the sects devoted to venerating Mary that began to spring up in the Eastern Roman Empire.

The pivotal figure in the growing Mary movement was Pulcheria, the eldest daughter of Arcadius, Emperor of the East. For more than a century, the Roman Empire had been divided for strategic reasons into the Western Empire and the Eastern Empire, ruled from Constantinople (known today as Istanbul, Turkey). The two halves were often ruled by different emperors, as was the case in Arcadius' and Pulcheria's time. When Arcadius died in 408 AD, the throne passed to his son, Theodosius II, who was only seven years old at the time. As his guardian and regent, Pulcheria became de facto ruler of the Empire of the East and assumed the title of Empress.

A devout Christian, Pulcheria dedicated her life to honoring Mary, taking a vow of lifelong virginity and persuading her sisters to do the same. In the beginning, there may have been a pragmatic reason for this; she would otherwise have been compelled to wed and thereby relinquish her imperial power to her husband. Be that as it may, she took her vow seriously. She transformed the imperial palace into a virtual monastery for Mary worshippers. She instituted a Virginity Festival for all chaste women on December 26. She also made Mary more visible in Constantinople by bringing various relics associated with her—her shroud, her belt, a portrait of her painted by the evangelist Luke—to the capital for public display. She built three churches to house these relics and instituted weekly ceremonies to honor Mary.

Pulcheria's ultimate act on behalf of Mary was calculated to exalt the virgin throughout the empire. It took place in the context of a theological dispute that was sweeping the land. Some writers had called Mary by the title *Theotokos,* usually translated as Mother of God, as early as the third century. But some Christians in Pulcheria's time, led by Nestorius, the Patriarch of Constantinople, objected to the title. No mortal creature, they said, could give birth to the divine; therefore, recognizing Mary as the Mother of God would be tantamount to declaring her a goddess.

To resolve the issue, Pulcheria's brother, the now-grown Emperor Theodosius, convened the Council of Ephesus in 431 AD. It was only the third time an ecumenical council had been held anywhere in Christendom. About 150 bishops from throughout the Christian world gathered in the hilltop city overlooking the Aegean Sea on the west coast of what is now Turkey. The choice of the site for the meeting was fitting because, according to legend, Mary had spent the last years of her life after Jesus' crucifixion in a small house in Ephesus.

Pulcheria led those who were in favor of the church's officially recognizing Mary as Theotokos. She succeeded in persuading the majority of the bishops to adopt her position, and Mary was officially recognized as Mother of God in a decision that was binding throughout the Christian world. Bishop Nestorius was stripped of his title and banished, first to Antioch and finally to a remote monastery in Egypt. An order was issued to burn his books and writings wherever they might be found.

One consequence of recognizing Mary as Mother of God was that it obligated Christians everywhere to venerate her by holding festivals in her honor and dedicating churches to her. This meant preaching the story of Mary and portraying events in her life on church walls. As their source, Christians drew on the Infancy Gospel of James. September 8 was designated as the Feast of the Birth of the Virgin, as noted on page 19, and many manuscripts of the Infancy Gospel bear the words "For

September 8." They must have been copied expressly to be read during the feast—notwithstanding Pope Gelasius' decree.

THE SECRET GOSPEL

Devotion to Mary spread from the East to the West in the seventh century, beginning in 614 AD when the Persians captured Jerusalem and many Christians fled to Rome, bringing their feasts and relics with them. Among the feasts were those celebrating the Birth of Mary and the Presentation of Mary in the Temple, both of which had their basis in the Infancy Gospel of James.

The story of Mary as related in the Infancy Gospel was kept alive through the Dark Ages in hymns and religious art. Mary has been the subject of more art works than any other woman in history. Paintings, mosaics, and book illustrations depict events that were never mentioned in the New Testament but originated with the Infancy Gospel.

The spread of Mary worship to the West meant that the Infancy Gospel, if translated into Latin, would have found a ready audience. But because the gospel was prohibited by the Roman church, some fancy footwork was required. The Infancy Gospel resurfaced in disguised form in the *Gospel of Pseudo-Matthew*. This book, which modern scholars date to the seventh or eighth

Paolo Uccello (1397-1475)
Presentation of the Virgin in the Temple,
Bocchineri Chapel, Prato

Written in the seventh or eighth century, the Gospel of Pseudo-Matthew adapts the stories in the Infancy Gospel, sometimes adding elaborate details. Pseudo-Matthew even names the specific number of steps Mary ascended in her presentation to the Temple—fifteen. Uccello's painting of her Presentation has exactly fifteen steps.

century, got its title because it purported to have been written in Hebrew by the evangelist Matthew and later translated into Latin by Saint Jerome—the very man who had rejected the original Infancy Gospel! The book incorporated much of the Infancy Gospel of James, though some parts were omitted and others were considerably expanded.

Toward the end of the ninth century another revised version of the Mary story appeared. The *Book of the Birth of Mary,* a largely reworked, shorter version of Pseudo-Matthew, omitted elements of the Infancy Gospel that contradicted biblical accounts, while elaborating on new material that had been added to Pseudo-Matthew.

Both revisions were relied upon by authors, historians, and poets in the tenth through twelfth centuries. Then, around 1230, three Dominican monks used these revisions in composing books that would spread the Marian legend to a much wider audience. Jean de Mailly compiled *Abbreviatio in gestis et meraculis sanctorum,* a book of the lives of the saints designed to be used for sermon preparation. In the chapter devoted to Mary, he

Fra Angelico (1387-1455)
Marriage of the Virgin, Museo di S. Marco, Florence

Whether Mary really married Joseph vacillates between the Gospel of Pseudo-Matthew (following the Infancy Gospel of James), which denies a real marriage, and the Book of the Birth of Mary, which assumes a real marriage. This painting by Fra Angelico takes the latter view and portrays Joseph and Mary getting married.

drew heavily on the Book of the Birth of Mary. In 1250, Barthélemy de Trente wrote a similar volume, *Epilogus in gesta sanctorum*, drawing on both the Birth of Mary and Pseudo-Matthew. Finally, about 1260, Jacobus de Voragine made use of both Jean de Mailly's and Barthélemy de Trente's books in writing his own book of the lives of the saints, *Legenda sanctorum,* commonly known as the Golden Legend.

It is through these Dominicans' works that Renaissance and Baroque artists learned of the life of Mary up to Jesus' birth. The result was an explosion of religious art depicting events that originally appeared in the Infancy Gospel of James—details of the Annunciation such as Mary holding a spindle of purple thread and encountering the angel beside a well or fountain; Joseph as an old man with a bald head, a gray beard, and a walking stick; pictures of Mary's parents, Anne and Joachim; the miraculous conception and birth of Mary; and Mary's childhood in the Temple in Jerusalem.

The influence on art of the Mary legend as originally set forth in the Infancy Gospel of James was remarkably widespread. An Armenian Bible from the late thirteenth century, for example, shows Mary holding the spindle of purple thread. A fourteenth-century mosaic at the Chora Monastery in Constantinople shows Mary standing at a fountain when the angel Gabriel greets her.

Giotto di Bondone (1266-1336)
The Meeting at the Golden Gate, Scrovegni Chapel, Padua

*Giotto's frescoes of the life of Mary are considered his masterpiece. This
one shows Mary's parents joyfully meeting at the Golden Gate of
Jerusalem after they learn that they will at last bear a child.*

In 1305, Mary was selected as the subject of a series of frescoes—murals painted on wet plaster so that
the paint would not peel or wear away with time. Those
frescoes would ultimately find a place among the most
influential works in the history of art. The site of the
paintings was a chapel that still stands today in Padua,
Italy. It is known as the Arena Chapel, because it was

built where an ancient Roman amphitheater had once stood, or the Cappella degli Scrovegni, after the man who built it. Enrico Scrovegni was the son and heir of the obscenely wealthy Reginaldo Scrovegni, whose unscrupulous moneylending activities were so widely known that Dante Alighieri's *Divine Comedy* named him specifically and consigned him to hell. The younger Scrovegni built the chapel for his family's use and dedicated it to Saint Mary of Charity to redeem his father's soul and save his own.

If you visit the Arena Chapel, you will find the walls completely covered with thirty-eight frescoes, arranged in three tiers. The murals are the work of Florentine painter and architect Giotto di Bondone, who is generally considered to be the father of Renaissance painting. He invented the technique of perspective—depicting three-dimensional scenes on two-dimensional surfaces. He reintroduced the naturalistic representation of humans and animals, which had been forgotten for centuries in Western art, and his paintings inspired such artists as Leonardo da Vinci and Michelangelo. Giotto's work can be seen in many of the great churches of Italy, including the Church of Saint Francis at Assisi and the Vatican in Rome, but art historians agree that the fullest expression of his genius was the series of frescoes in the Arena Chapel.

The top tier of the chapel's frescoes depicts events in the life of Mary, arranged in chronological order. The series begins, as does the Infancy Gospel of James, with Joachim and Anne. One shows Joachim being expelled from the Temple because he is childless (page 63). In another, Anne is being told by an angel that she will at last give birth to a child (page 70), and in the next, Joachim receives the same angelic message (page 12). Then comes the couple's joyous embrace outside the Golden Gate of Jerusalem (page 37). The series goes on to depict Anne giving birth to Mary (page 19), Mary's presentation to the Temple at age three (page 77), an angel feeding Mary in the Temple, priests praying over staffs to decide who will wed Mary (page 81), and her being given to Joseph (page 25).

It is obvious that Giotto's work in the Arena Chapel was inspired—if not by the forbidden Infancy Gospel of James itself—by the Golden Legend or one of the other watered-down versions edited by Dominican monks in the previous century. In fact, all sixteen frescoes in the top tier depict events that originally appeared in the Infancy Gospel, and of those, only three relate to events mentioned in the New Testament gospels. Like so many other aspects of Giotto's work, his extensive use of this subject matter inspired the Renaissance and Baroque

Raphael (1483-1520)
The Canigiani Holy Family,
Alte Pinakothek, Munich

*Artists traditionally portray Joseph as an older man
with a bald head and gray beard. But the Bible says nothing
of Joseph's advanced age—these details derive instead from the
Infancy Gospel of James and its later adaptations.*

artists that would come later, popularizing the Mary legend in religious paintings for the next three centuries.

For instance, German painter Stefan Lochner's masterpiece, *The Marriage of the Virgin,* now in a private collection, shows Joseph as an elderly man with a bald head and a long, flowing white beard. Painted between 1505 and 1510, Venetian artist Giorgione's *Adoration of the Shepherds* also shows Joseph with a bald head and white beard. It can be seen today in the National Gallery of Art in Washington, DC. In 1507, the great Italian Renaissance artist and poet Raphael painted *The Canigiani Holy Family* (page 40). Now in the Alte Pinakothek art museum in Munich, the work shows Mary, Elizabeth, and their children Jesus and John the Baptist. The elderly Joseph looms over them, leaning on his staff with his eyes downcast so that his shiny bald head is his most prominent feature.

Leonardo da Vinci's painting *The Virgin and Child with Saint Anne,* created sometime between 1507 and 1513, hangs in the Louvre in Paris today (page 10). Most Christians of da Vinci's time would immediately recognize Anne, Mary's mother, in the background— even though Anne does not appear anywhere in the New Testament.

The list of paintings goes on. *The Birth of Jesus* by Guidoccio Cozzarelli, another early-sixteenth-century

Italian artist, also shows Joseph as bald with a long gray beard; it is now part of the Perkins Collection in Assisi. An elderly Joseph appears in *The Flight into Egypt* by Jacopo Tintoretto, painted between 1583 and 1587, depicting Mary on a donkey with the bald Joseph trailing behind; it hangs in the Scuola Grande di San Rocco in Venice. In the great Dutch Baroque painter Rembrandt van Rijn's *The Presentation of Jesus in the Temple,* painted in 1631 and now in the Kuntsthalle museum in Hamburg, we see an exceptionally elderly looking Joseph, bent and with a long beard, holding the infant Jesus.

Though the written words of the Infancy Gospel of James seemed lost, thanks to these writers and artists the story it told was never forgotten.

THE GOSPEL RESURFACES

And what of the Infancy Gospel of James itself, the basis of all these later books and paintings? Despite the Western church's prohibition, many manuscripts of the Infancy Gospel of James survived. Indeed, over 140 Greek manuscripts of this gospel are known to exist, although for a long time the oldest one was only from the tenth century. That situation changed significantly with the publication in 1958 of Bodmer Papyrus V, a fourth-century copy which is now the earliest manuscript of this gospel. Its text is not only 600 years earlier than the previous earliest manuscript but is also superior in many passages. It is, therefore, now possible for the first time to provide a significantly more accurate translation of this gospel in this volume along with every mention of Mary contained in the canonical New Testament.

The timing of the gospel's reappearance is something of a marvel in itself. In the last years of the twentieth century and the dawn of the new millennium, the veneration of Mary is stronger than ever before in history.

From Clearwater, Florida, to Medjugorje, Bosnia-Herzegovina, 386 miraculous apparitions of Mary were reported in the twentieth century. After rigorous scrutiny, the Catholic Church has rejected the authenticity of only seventy-nine of them.

Five million people a year visit Lourdes, France, to bathe in the waters whose healing effects are attributed to Mary's powers.

Two *billion* Hail Marys are said on earth every day.

Since 1993, millions of Roman Catholics have petitioned the Pope to proclaim a new dogma that would effectively add Mary to the Holy Trinity. At last count, the petition has been signed by more than six million people in 148 countries, including 42 cardinals, more than 500 bishops, and Mother Teresa.

It appears that Mary's time has come.

This is her story . . .

Mary in the New Testament

While most people believe that there is ample information about Mary in the Bible, the number of New Testament references to her actually total fewer than two dozen. Many of the details that form the folklore of Mary come from other sources, particularly the Infancy Gospel of James. As startling evidence of how little Mary material actually appears in the canonical Gospels, here are the relevant passages from the Bible.

MATTHEW 1: 18–25

NOW THE BIRTH OF JESUS THE MESSIAH took place in this way. When his mother Mary had been engaged to Joseph, but before they lived together, she was found to be with child from the Holy Spirit. Her husband Joseph, being a righteous man and unwilling to expose her to public disgrace, planned to dismiss her quietly. But just when he had resolved to do this, an angel of the Lord appeared to him in a dream and said, "Joseph, son of David, do not be afraid to take Mary as your wife, for the child conceived in her is from the Holy Spirit. She will bear a son, and you are to name him Jesus, for he will save his people from their sins."

All this took place to fulfill what had been spoken by the Lord through the prophet: "Look, the virgin shall conceive and bear a son, and they shall name him Emmanuel," which means, "God is with us." When Joseph awoke from sleep, he did as the angel of the Lord commanded him; he took her as his wife, but had no marital relations with her until she had borne a son; and he named him Jesus.

MATTHEW 2: 11–15

O N ENTERING THE HOUSE, THE WISE MEN saw the child with Mary his mother; and they knelt down and paid him homage. Then, opening their treasure chests, they offered him gifts of gold, frankincense, and myrrh. And having been warned in a dream not to return to Herod, they left for their own country by another road.

Now after they had left, an angel of the Lord appeared to Joseph in a dream and said, "Get up, take the child and his mother, and flee to Egypt, and remain there until I tell you; for Herod is about to search for the child, to destroy him."

Then Joseph got up, took the child and his mother by night, and went to Egypt, and remained there until the death of Herod. This was to fulfill what had been spoken by the Lord through the prophet, "Out of Egypt I have called my son."

Lucas Cranach the Elder (1472-1553)
Rest on the Flight into Egypt, Staatliche Museen, Berlin

*The flight into Egypt, merely mentioned in the Bible, is greatly
elaborated in the Gospel of Pseudo-Matthew. One scene from
Pseudo-Matthew that's especially popular with artists is the holy
family's stop to rest on the way.*

MATTHEW 12: 46–50

WHILE HE WAS STILL SPEAKING TO THE crowds, his mother and his brothers were standing outside, wanting to speak to him. Someone told him, "Look, your mother and your brothers are standing outside, wanting to speak to you." But to the one who had told him this, Jesus replied, "Who is my mother, and who are my brothers?" And pointing to his disciples, he said, "Here are my mother and my brothers! For whoever does the will of my Father in heaven is my brother and sister and mother."

MARK 6: 1–3

H E LEFT THAT PLACE AND CAME TO HIS hometown, and his disciples followed him. On the sabbath he began to teach in the synagogue, and many who heard him were astounded. They said, "Where did this man get all this? What is this wisdom that has been given to him? What deeds of power are being done by his hands! Is not this the carpenter, the son of Mary and brother of James and Joses and Judas and Simon, and are not his sisters here with us?" And they took offense at him.

LUKE 1: 26–56

IN THE SIXTH MONTH THE ANGEL GABRIEL was sent by God to a town in Galilee called Nazareth, to a virgin engaged to a man whose name was Joseph, of the house of David. The virgin's name was Mary. And he came to her and said, "Greetings, favored one! The Lord is with you." But she was much perplexed by his words and pondered what sort of greeting this might be.

The angel said to her, "Do not be afraid, Mary, for you have found favor with God. And now, you will conceive in your womb and bear a son, and you will call him Jesus. He will be great, and will be called the Son of the Most High, and the Lord God will give to him the throne of his ancestor David. He will reign over the house of Jacob forever, and of his kingdom there will be no end."

Mary said to the angels, "How can this be, since I am a virgin?" The angel said to her, "The Holy Spirit will come upon you, and the power of the Most High will overshadow you; therefore the child to be born will be holy; he will be called Son of God. And now, your relative Elizabeth in her old age has also conceived a son; and this is the sixth month for her who was said to be barren. For nothing will be impossible with God." Then Mary said, "Here am I, the servant of the Lord; let it be with me according to your word." Then the angel departed from her.

In those days Mary set out and went with haste to a Judean town in the hill country, where she entered the house of Zechariah and greeted Elizabeth. When Elizabeth heard Mary's greeting, the child leaped in her womb. And Elizabeth was filled with the Holy Spirit and exclaimed with a loud cry, "Blessed are you among women, and blessed is the fruit of your womb. And why has this happened to me, that the mother of my Lord comes to me? For as soon as I heard the sound of your greeting, the child in my womb leaped for joy. And blessed is she who believed that there would be a fulfillment of what was spoken to her by the Lord."

And Mary said, "My soul magnifies the Lord and my spirit rejoices in God my Savior, for he has looked with favor on the lowliness of his servant. Surely, from now on all generations will call me blessed; for the Mighty One has done great things for me, and holy is his name. His mercy is for those who fear him from generation to generation. He has shown strength with his arm; he has scattered the proud in the thoughts of their hearts. He has brought down the powerful from their thrones, and lifted up the lowly; He has filled the hungry with good things, and sent the rich away empty. He has helped his servant Israel, in remembrance of his mercy, according to the promise he made to our ancestors, to Abraham and to his descendants forever." And Mary remained with her about three months and then returned to her home.

LUKE 2: 5–7

H E WENT TO BE REGISTERED WITH MARY, to whom he was engaged and who was expecting a child. While they were there, the time came for her to deliver her child. And she gave birth to her firstborn son and wrapped him in bands of cloth, and laid him in a manger, because there was no place for them in the inn.

Martin Schongauer (1435-1491) *The Birth of Christ*,
Gemäldegalerie, Staatliche Museen, Berlin

*The Gospel of Pseudo-Matthew's most popular addition to the story
begun in the Infancy Gospel of James is the placement of an ox and ass
at the stable where Jesus is born. These animals appear in many
paintings, including this one by Schongauer.*

LUKE 2: 15–19

WHEN THE ANGELS HAD LEFT THEM AND gone into heaven, the shepherds said to one another, "Let us go now to Bethlehem and see this thing that has taken place, which the Lord has made known to us." So they went with haste and found Mary and Joseph, and the child lying in the manger. When they saw this, they made known what had been told them about this child; and all who heard it were amazed at what the shepherds told them. But Mary treasured all these words and pondered them in her heart.

JOHN 2: 1–7

ON THE THIRD DAY THERE WAS A WEDDING in Cana of Galilee, and the mother of Jesus was there. Jesus and his disciples had also been invited to the wedding. When the wine gave out, the mother of Jesus said to him, "They have no wine." And Jesus said to her, "Woman, what concern is that to you and to me? My hour has not yet come." His mother said to the servants, "Do whatever he tells you." Now standing there were six stone water jars for the Jewish rites of purification, each holding twenty or thirty gallons. Jesus said to them, "Fill the jars with water." And they filled them up to the brim.

JOHN 19: 25–27

AND THAT IS WHAT THE SOLDIERS DID. Meanwhile, standing near the cross of Jesus were his mother, and his mother's sister, Mary the wife of Clopas, and Mary Magdalene. When Jesus saw his mother and the disciple whom he loved standing beside her, he said to his mother, "Woman, here is your son." Then he said to the disciple, "Here is your mother." And from that hour the disciple took her into his own home.

ACTS 1:14

ALL THE APOSTLES WERE OF ONE MIND devoting themselves to prayer along with some women, including Mary the mother of Jesus, and his brothers.

GALATIANS 4:44

GOD SENT HIS SON, BORN OF A WOMAN, born under law.

Infancy
Gospel
of James

◆ 1 ◆

ACCORDING TO THE RECORDS OF THE twelve tribes of Israel, there once was a very rich man named Joachim. He always doubled the gifts he offered to the Lord, and would say to himself, "One gift, representing my prosperity, will be for all the people; the other, offered for forgiveness, will be my sin-offering to the Lord God."

Now the great day of the Lord was approaching, and the people of Israel were offering their gifts. And Reubel confronted Joachim and said, "You're not allowed to offer your gifts first because you haven't produced an Israelite child."

And Joachim became very upset and went to the book of the twelve tribes of the people, saying to himself, "I'm going to check the book of the twelve tribes of Israel to see whether I'm the only one in Israel who hasn't produced a child." And he searched the records and found that all the righteous people in Israel did indeed

Giotto di Bondone (1266-1336)
The Expulsion of Joachim from the Temple, Scrovegni Chapel, Padua

Joachim is expelled from the Temple of Jerusalem because he alone of all the Israelites has yet to father a child.

have children. And he remembered the patriarch Abraham because in his last days the Lord God had given him a son, Isaac.

And so he continued to be very upset and did not see his wife but banished himself to the wilderness and pitched his tent there. And Joachim fasted forty days and forty nights. He would say to himself, "I will not go back for food or drink until the Lord my God visits me. Prayer will be my food and drink."

⋄2⋄

NOW HIS WIFE ANNE WAS MOURNING and lamenting on two counts: "I lament my widowhood and I lament my childlessness."

The great day of the Lord approached, however, and Juthine her slave said to her, "How long are you going to humble yourself? Look, the great day of the Lord has arrived, and you're not supposed to mourn. Rather, take this headband which the mistress of the workshop gave to me but which I'm not allowed to wear because I'm your slave and because it bears a royal insignia."

And Anne said, "Get away from me! I won't take it. The Lord God has greatly shamed me. Maybe a trickster has given you this, and you've come to make me share in your sin."

And Juthine the slave replied, "Should I curse you just because you haven't paid any attention to me? The Lord God has made your womb sterile so you won't bear any children for Israel."

Anne, too, became very upset. She took off her mourning clothes, washed her face, and put on her wedding dress. Then in the middle of the afternoon, she went down to her garden to take a walk. She spied a laurel tree and sat down under it. After resting, she prayed to the Lord: "O God of my ancestors, bless me and hear my prayer, just as you blessed our mother Sarah and gave her a son, Isaac."

◆3◆

AND ANNE LOOKED UP TOWARD THE SKY and saw a nest of sparrows in the laurel tree. And immediately Anne began to lament, saying to herself:

"Poor me! Who gave birth to me? What sort of womb bore me? For I was born under a curse in the eyes of the people of Israel. And I've been reviled and mocked and banished from the temple of the Lord my God.

"Poor me! What am I like? I am not like the birds of the sky, because even the birds of the sky reproduce in your presence, O Lord.

"Poor me! What am I like? I am not like the domestic animals, because even the domestic animals bear young in your presence, O Lord.

"Poor me! What am I like? I am not like the wild animals of the earth, because even the animals of the earth reproduce in your presence, O Lord.

"Poor me! What am I like? I am not like these waters, because even these waters are productive in your presence, O Lord.

"Poor me! What am I like? I am not like this earth, because even the earth produces its crops in season and blesses you, O Lord."

•4•

SUDDENLY A MESSENGER OF THE LORD appeared to her and said to her: "Anne, Anne, the Lord God has heard your prayer. You will conceive and give birth, and your child will be talked about all over the world."

And Anne said, "As the Lord God lives, whether I give birth to a boy or a girl, I'll offer it as a gift to the Lord my God, and it will serve him its whole life."

And right then two messengers reported to her: "Look, your husband Joachim is coming with his flocks. You see, a messenger of the Lord had come down to Joachim and said, 'Joachim, Joachim, the Lord God has heard your prayer. Get down from there. Look, your wife Anne is pregnant.'"

And Joachim went down right away and summoned his shepherds with these instructions: "Bring me ten lambs without spot or blemish, and the ten lambs will be for the Lord God. Also, bring me twelve tender calves, and

Giotto di Bondone (1266-1336)
The Annunciation to Saint Anne, Scrovegni Chapel, Padua

Anne had despaired of bearing a child, but a
heavenly messenger tells her that she is pregnant.
She vows to give the child to God.

the twelve calves will be for the priests and the council of elders. Also, one hundred goats, and the one hundred goats will be for the whole people."

And so Joachim was coming with his flocks, while Anne stood at the gate. Then she spotted Joachim approaching with his flocks and rushed out and threw her arms around his neck and said, "Now I know that the Lord God has blessed me greatly. This widow is no longer a widow, and I, once childless, am now pregnant!"

And Joachim rested the first day at home.

⬧5⬧

BUT ON THE NEXT DAY, AS HE WAS presenting his gifts, he thought to himself, "If the Lord God has really been merciful to me, the polished disc on the priest's headband will make it clear to me." And so Joachim was presenting his gifts and paying attention to the priest's headband until he went up to the altar of the Lord. And he saw no sin in it. And Joachim said, "Now I know that the Lord God has been merciful to me and has forgiven me all my sins." And he came down from the temple of the Lord acquitted and went back home.

And so her pregnancy came to term, and in the ninth month Anne gave birth. And she said to the midwife, "Is it a boy or girl?"

And her midwife said, "A girl."

And Anne said, "I have been greatly honored this day." Then the midwife put the child to bed.

When, however, the prescribed days were completed, Anne cleansed herself of the flow of blood. And she offered her breast to the infant and gave her the name Mary.

◆6◆

DAY BY DAY THE INFANT GREW STRONGER. When she was six months old, her mother put her on the ground to see if she could stand. She walked seven steps and went to her mother's arms. Then her mother picked her up and said, "As the Lord my God lives, you will never walk on this ground again until I take you into the temple of the Lord."

And so she turned her bedroom into a sanctuary and did not permit anything profane or unclean to pass the child's lips. She sent for the undefiled daughters of the Hebrews, and they kept her amused.

Now the child had her first birthday, and Joachim gave a great banquet and invited the high priests, priests, scholars, council of elders, and all the people of Israel. Joachim presented the child to the priests, and they blessed her: "God of our fathers, bless this child and give her a name which will be on the lips of future generations forever."

And everyone said, "So be it. Amen."

He presented her to the high priests, and they blessed her: "Most high God, look on this child and bless her with the ultimate blessing, one which cannot be surpassed."

Her mother then took her up to the sanctuary—the bedroom—and gave her breast to the child. And Anne composed a song for the Lord God:

"I will sing a sacred song to the Lord my God because he has visited me and taken away the disgrace attributed to me by my enemies. The Lord my God has given me the fruit of his righteousness, single yet manifold before him. Who will announce to the sons of Reubel that Anne has a child at her breast? 'Listen, listen, you twelve tribes of Israel: Anne has a child at her breast!'"

Anne made her rest in the bedroom—the sanctuary—and then went out and began serving her guests. When the banquet was over, they left in good spirits and praised the God of Israel.

◆7◆

MANY MONTHS PASSED, BUT WHEN THE child reached two years of age, Joachim said, "Let's take her up to the temple of the Lord, so that we can keep the promise we made, or else the Lord will be angry with us and our gift will be unacceptable."

And Anne said, "Let's wait until she is three, so she won't miss her father or mother."

And Joachim agreed: "Let's wait."

When the child turned three years of age, Joachim said, "Let's send for the undefiled Hebrew daughters. Let them each take a lamp and light it, so the child won't turn back and have her heart captivated by things outside the Lord's temple." And this is what they did until the time they ascended to the Lord's temple.

The priest welcomed her, kissed her, and blessed her: "The Lord God has exalted your name among all generations. In you the Lord will disclose his redemption to the people of Israel during the last days."

And he sat her down on the third step of the altar, and the Lord God showered favor on her. And she danced, and the whole house of Israel loved her.

Giotto di Bondone (1266-1336)
The Presentation of Mary to the Temple, Scrovegni Chapel, Padua

*When she is only three years old, Mary's parents take her
to live in the Temple of Jerusalem, where she dwells in the purest
surroundings imaginable, fed by an angel.*

◆8◆

HER PARENTS LEFT FOR HOME, MARVELING and praising and glorifying the Lord God because the child did not look back at them. And Mary lived in the temple of the Lord. She was fed there like a dove, receiving her food from the hand of a heavenly messenger.

When she turned twelve, however, there was a meeting of the priests. "Look," they said, "Mary has turned twelve in the temple of the Lord. What should we do with her so she won't pollute the sanctuary of the Lord our God?" And they said to the high priest, "You stand at the altar of the Lord. Enter and pray about her, and we'll do whatever the Lord God discloses to you."

And so the high priest took the vestment with the twelve bells, entered the Holy of Holies, and began to pray about her. And suddenly a messenger of the Lord appeared: "Zechariah, Zechariah, go out and assemble the widowers of the people and have them each bring a staff. She will become the wife of the one to whom the Lord God shows a sign." And so heralds covered the surrounding territory of Judea. The trumpet of the Lord sounded and all the widowers came running.

◆9◆

JOSEPH, TOO, THREW DOWN HIS CARPENTER'S ax and left for the meeting. When they had all gathered, they went to the high priest with their staffs. After the high priest had collected everyone's staff, he entered the temple and began to pray. When he had finished his prayer, he took the staffs and went out and began to give them back to each one. But there was no sign on any of them. Joseph got the last staff. Suddenly a dove came out of this staff and perched on Joseph's head. "Joseph, Joseph," the high priest said, "you've been chosen by lot to take the virgin of the Lord into your care and protection."

But Joseph objected: "I already have sons and I'm an old man; she's only a young woman. I'm afraid that I'll become the butt of jokes among the people of Israel."

And the high priest responded, "Joseph, fear the Lord your God and remember what God did to Dathan, Abiron, and Kore: the earth was

Giotto di Bondone (1266-1336)
The Rods Brought to the Temple, Scrovegni Chapel, Padua

The priests of the Temple decide they cannot keep Mary any longer once she reaches womanhood at the age of twelve. They summon the widowers of Jerusalem to bring staffs to the Temple, hoping God will send a sign to show which one Mary should marry.

split open and they were all swallowed up because of their objection. So now, Joseph, you ought to take heed so that the same thing won't happen to your family."

And so out of fear Joseph took her into his care and protection. He said to her, "Mary, I've gotten you from the temple of the Lord, but now I'm leaving you at home. I'm going away to build houses, but I'll come back to you. The Lord will protect you."

·10·

MEANWHILE, THERE WAS A COUNCIL OF the priests, who agreed: "Let's make a veil for the temple of the Lord."

And the high priest said, "Summon the true virgins for me from the tribe of David." And so the temple assistants left and searched everywhere and found seven. And the high priest then remembered the girl Mary, that she, too, was from the tribe of David and was pure in God's eyes. And so the temple assistants went out and got her.

And they took the maidens into the temple of the Lord. And the high priest said, "Cast lots for me to decide who'll spin which threads for the veil: the gold, the white, the linen, the silk, the violet, the scarlet, and the true purple."

And the true purple and scarlet threads fell to Mary. And she took them and returned home. Now it was at this time that Zechariah became mute, and Samuel took his place until Zechariah regained his speech. Meanwhile, Mary had taken up the scarlet and was spinning it.

◆ 11 ◆

AND SHE TOOK HER WATER JAR AND WENT
out to fill it with water. Suddenly there
was a voice saying to her, "Greetings, favored
one! The Lord is with you. Blessed are you
among women." Mary began looking around,
both right and left, to see where the voice was
coming from. She became terrified and went
home. After putting the water jar down and taking up the purple thread, she sat down on her
chair and began to spin.

A heavenly messenger suddenly stood
before her: "Don't be afraid, Mary. You see,
you've found favor in the sight of the Lord of all.
You will conceive by means of his word."

But as she listened, Mary was doubtful and
said, "If I actually conceive by the Lord, the living God, will I also give birth the way women
usually do?"

And the messenger of the Lord replied,
"No, Mary, because the power of God will overshadow you. Therefore, the child to be born will

be called holy, a son of the Most High. And you will name him Jesus—the name means 'he will save his people from their sins.'"

And Mary said, "Here I am, the Lord's slave before him. I pray that all you've told me comes true."

◆ 12 ◆

AND SHE FINISHED SPINNING THE purple and the scarlet thread and took her work up to the high priest. The high priest accepted them and praised her and said, "Mary, the Lord God has extolled your name and so you'll be blessed by all the generations of the earth."

Mary rejoiced and left to visit her relative Elizabeth. She knocked at the door. Elizabeth heard her, tossed aside the scarlet thread, ran to the door, and opened it for her. And she blessed her and said, "Who am I that the mother of my Lord should visit me? You see, the baby inside me has jumped for joy and blessed you."

But Mary forgot the mysteries which the heavenly messenger Gabriel had spoken, and she looked up to heaven and said, "Who am I, Lord, that every generation on earth will bless me?"

She spent three months with Elizabeth. And day by day her womb kept swelling. And so

Mary became frightened, returned home, and hid from the people of Israel. She was sixteen years old when these mysterious things happened to her.

◆13◆

SHE WAS IN HER SIXTH MONTH WHEN ONE day Joseph came home from his building projects, entered his house, and found her pregnant. He struck himself in the face, threw himself to the ground on sackcloth, and began to cry bitterly: "What sort of face should I present to the Lord God? What prayer can I say on her behalf since I received her as a virgin from the temple of the Lord God and didn't protect her? Who has set this trap for me? Who has done this evil deed in my house? Who has lured this virgin away from me and violated her? The story of Adam has been repeated in my case, hasn't it? For just as Adam was praying when the serpent came and found Eve alone, deceived her, and corrupted her, so the same thing has happened to me."

So Joseph got up from the sackcloth and summoned her and said to her, "God has taken a special interest in you—how could you have done this? Have you forgotten the Lord your

God? Why have you brought shame on your-self, you who were raised in the Holy of Holies and fed by a heavenly messenger?"

But she began to cry bitter tears: "I am innocent. I haven't had sex with any man."

And Joseph said to her, "Then where did the child you're carrying come from?"

And she replied, "As the Lord my God lives, I don't know where it came from."

⬥14⬥

AND JOSEPH BECAME VERY FRIGHTENED and no longer spoke with her as he pondered what he was going to do with her. And Joseph said to himself, "If I try to cover up her sin, I'll end up going against the law of the Lord. But if I disclose her condition to the people of Israel, I'm afraid that the child inside her might be heaven-sent and I'll end up handing innocent blood over to a death sentence. So what should I do with her? I know, I'll divorce her quietly."

But when night came a messenger of the Lord suddenly appeared to him in a dream and said: "Don't be afraid of this girl, because the child in her is the holy spirit's doing. She will have a son and you will name him Jesus—the name means 'he will save his people from their sins.'" And Joseph got up from his sleep and praised the God of Israel who had given him this favor. And so he began to protect the girl.

·15·

THEN ANNAS THE SCHOLAR CAME TO HIM and said to him, "Joseph, why haven't you attended our assembly?"

And he replied to him, "Because I was worn out from the trip and rested my first day home."

Then Annas turned and saw that Mary was pregnant.

He left in a hurry for the high priest and said to him, "You remember Joseph, don't you—the man you yourself vouched for? Well, he's committed a serious offense."

And the high priest asked, "In what way?"

"Joseph has violated the virgin he received from the temple of the Lord," he replied. "He had his way with her and hasn't disclosed his action to the people of Israel."

And the high priest asked him, "Has Joseph really done this?"

And he replied, "Send temple assistants and you'll find the virgin pregnant."

And so the temple assistants went and found her just as Annas had reported, and then they brought her, along with Joseph, to the court.

"Mary, why have you done this?" the high priest asked her. "Why have you humiliated yourself? Have you forgotten the Lord your God, you who were raised in the Holy of the Holies and fed by heavenly messengers? You of all people, you who heard their hymns and danced for them—why have you done this?"

And she wept bitterly: "As the Lord God lives, I stand innocent before him. Believe me, I've not had sex with any man."

And the high priest said, "Joseph, why have you done this?"

And Joseph said, "As the Lord lives, I am innocent where she is concerned."

And the high priest said, "Don't perjure yourself, but tell the truth. You've had your way with her and haven't disclosed this action to the people of Israel. And you haven't humbled yourself under God's mighty hand, so that your offspring might be blessed."

But Joseph was silent.

·16·

THEN THE HIGH PRIEST SAID, "RETURN THE virgin you received from the temple of the Lord."

And Joseph burst into tears. . . .

And the high priest said, "I'm going to give you the Lord's drink test, and it will disclose your sin clearly to both of you."

And the high priest took the water and made Joseph drink it and sent him into the wilderness, but he returned unharmed. And he made the girl drink it, too, and sent her into the wilderness. She also came back unharmed. And everybody was surprised because their sin had not been revealed. And so the high priest said, "If the Lord God has not exposed your sin, then neither do I condemn you." And he dismissed them. Joseph took Mary and returned home celebrating and praising the God of Israel.

◆ 17 ◆

NOW AN ORDER CAME FROM THE EMPEROR Augustus that everybody in Bethlehem of Judea be enrolled in the census. And Joseph wondered, "I'll enroll my sons, but what am I going to do with this girl? How will I enroll her? As my wife? I'm ashamed to do that. As my daughter? The people of Israel know she's not my daughter. How this matter is to be decided depends on the Lord."

And so he saddled his donkey and had her get on it. His son led it and Samuel tailed along behind. As they neared the three mile marker, Joseph turned around and saw that she was sulking. And he said to himself, "Perhaps the baby she is carrying is causing her discomfort." Joseph turned around again and saw her laughing and said to her, "Mary, what's going on with you? One minute I see you're laughing and the next minute you're sulking."

And she replied, "Joseph, it's because I imagine two peoples in front of me, one weeping and mourning and the other celebrating and jumping for joy."

Halfway through the trip Mary said to him, "Joseph, help me down from the donkey—the child inside me is about to be born."

And he helped her down and said to her, "Where will I take you to give you some privacy, since this place is out in the open?"

·18·

H E FOUND A CAVE NEARBY AND TOOK HER
inside. He stationed his sons to guard her
and went to look for a Hebrew midwife in the
country around Bethlehem.

"Now I, Joseph, was walking along and yet
not going anywhere. I looked up at the vault of
the sky and saw it standing still, and then at the
clouds and saw them paused in amazement,
and the birds of the sky suspended in midair. As
I looked on the earth, I saw a bowl lying there
and workers reclining around it with their hands
in the bowl; some were chewing and yet did not
chew; some were picking up something to eat
and yet did not pick it up; and some were putting food in their mouths and yet did not do so.
Instead, they were all looking upward.

"I saw sheep being driven along and yet the
sheep stood still; the shepherd was lifting his
hand to strike them, and yet his hand remained
raised. Then I observed the current of the river
and saw goats with their mouths in the water

and yet they were not drinking. Then all of a
sudden everything and everybody went on with
what they had been doing."

·19·

"THEN I SAW A WOMAN COMING DOWN from the hill country, and she asked, 'Where are you going, sir?'

"And I replied, 'I'm looking for a Hebrew midwife.'

"She inquired, 'Are you an Israelite?'

"I told her, 'Yes.'

"And she said, 'And who's the one having a baby in the cave?'

"I replied, 'My fiancée.'

"And she continued, 'She isn't your wife?'

"I said to her, 'She is Mary, who was raised in the temple of the Lord; I obtained her by lot as my wife. But she's not really my wife; she's pregnant by the holy spirit.'

"The midwife said, 'Really?'"

Joseph responded, "Come and see."

And the midwife went with him. As they stood in front of the cave, a dark cloud overshadowed it. The midwife said, "I've really been privileged, because today my eyes have seen a miracle in that salvation has come to Israel."

Robert Campin (1375-1444)
Adoration of the Shepherds, Musée des Beaux-Arts, Dijon

*The Infancy Gospel of James tells of two midwives—one believing,
the other skeptical—who arrive shortly after the birth of Mary.
The Latin legend under the midwife in this painting translates as
"A virgin has given birth to a son," words that recall the confession of
the midwife in the Infancy Gospel.*

Suddenly the cloud withdrew from the cave and an intense light appeared inside the cave, so that their eyes could not bear to look. And a little later that light receded until an infant became visible; he took the breast of his mother Mary.

Then the midwife shouted: "What a great day this is for me because I've seen this new miracle!"

And the midwife left the cave and met Salome and said to her, "Salome, Salome, let me tell you about a new marvel: a virgin has given birth, and you know that's impossible!"

And Salome replied, "As the Lord my God lives, unless I insert my finger and examine her, I will never believe that a virgin has given birth."

◆20◆

THE MIDWIFE ENTERED AND SAID, "MARY, position yourself for an examination. You are facing a serious test."

And so Mary, when she heard these instructions, positioned herself, and Salome inserted her finger into Mary. And then Salome cried aloud and said, "Woe is me because of my transgression and my disbelief; I have put the living God on trial. Look! My hand is disappearing! It's being consumed by flames!"

Then Salome fell on her knees in the presence of the Lord, with these words, "God of my ancestors, remember me because I'm a descendant of Abraham, Isaac, and Jacob. Don't make an example of me for the people of Israel, but give me a place among the poor again. You yourself know, Lord, that I've been healing people in your name and have been receiving my payment from you."

And suddenly a messenger from the Lord appeared, saying to her, "Salome, Salome, the

Lord of all has heard your prayer. Hold out your hand to the child and pick him up, and then you'll have salvation and joy."

Salome approached the child and picked him up with these words, "I'll worship him because he's been born to be king of Israel." And Salome was instantly healed and left the cave vindicated.

Then a voice said abruptly, "Salome, Salome, don't report the marvels you've seen until the child goes to Jerusalem."

·21·

JOSEPH WAS ABOUT READY TO DEPART FOR
Judea when a great uproar was about to take
place in Bethlehem in Judea. It all started when
magi came inquiring, "Where is the newborn
king of the Judeans? We're here because we saw
his star in the East and have come to pay him
homage."

When Herod heard about their visit, he was
terrified and sent agents to the magi. He also
sent for the high priests and questioned them in
his palace: "What's been written about the
Anointed? Where is he supposed to be born?"

They said to him, "In Bethlehem, Judea,
that's what the scriptures say." And he dismissed them.

Then he questioned the magi: "What sign
have you seen regarding the one who has been
born king?"

And the magi said, "We saw a star of exceptional brilliance in the sky, and it so dimmed
the other stars that they disappeared. Con-

sequently, we know that a king was born for Israel. And we have come to pay him homage."

Herod instructed them: "Go and begin your search, and if you find him, report back to me, so that I can also go and pay him homage."

The magi departed. And there it was: the star they had seen in the East led them on until they came to the cave; then the star stopped directly above the head of the child. After the magi saw him with his mother Mary, they took gifts out of their pouches—gold, pure incense, and myrrh.

Since they had been advised by the heavenly messenger not to go into Judea, they returned to their country by another route.

•22•

WHEN HEROD REALIZED HE HAD BEEN duped by the astrologers, he flew into a rage and dispatched his executioners with instructions to kill all the infants two years old and younger.

When Mary heard that the infants were being killed, she was frightened and took her child, wrapped him in strips of cloth, and placed him in a feeding trough used by cattle.

As for Elizabeth, when she heard that they were looking for John, she took him and went up into the hill country. She kept searching for a place to hide him, but there was none to be had. Then she groaned and said out loud, "Mountain of God, please take in a mother with her child." You see, Elizabeth was unable to keep on climbing because her nerve failed her. But suddenly the mountain was split open and let them in. This mountain allowed the light to shine through to her, since a messenger of the Lord was with them for protection.

·23·

HEROD, THOUGH, KEPT LOOKING FOR JOHN and sent his agents to Zechariah serving at the altar with this message for him: "Where have you hidden your son?"

But he answered them, "I am a minister of God, attending to his temple. How should I know where my son is?"

And so the agents left and reported all this to Herod, who became angry and said, "Is his son going to rule over Israel?"

And he sent his agents back with this message for him: "Tell me the truth. Where is your son? Don't you know that I have your life in my power?"

And the agents went and reported this message to him.

Zechariah answered, "I am a martyr for God. Take my life. The Lord, though, will receive my spirit because you are shedding innocent blood at the entrance to the temple of the Lord."

And so at daybreak Zechariah was murdered, but the people of Israel did not know that
he had been murdered.

·24·

AT THE HOUR OF FORMAL GREETINGS THE priests departed, but Zechariah did not meet and bless them as was customary. And so the priests waited around for Zechariah, to greet him with prayer and to praise the Most High God.

But when he did not show up, they all became fearful. One of them, however, summoned up his courage, entered the sanctuary, and saw dried blood next to the Lord's altar. And a voice said, "Zechariah has been murdered! His blood will not be cleaned up until his avenger appears."

When he heard this utterance he was afraid and went out and reported to the priests what he had seen and heard. They also summoned up their courage, entered, and saw what had happened. The panels of the temple cried out, and the priests ripped their robes from top to bottom. They did not find his corpse, but they did find his blood, now turned to stone. They were afraid and went out and reported to the people that Zechariah had been murdered. When all the tribes of the people heard this, they began to mourn; and they beat their breasts for three days and three nights.

After three days, however, the priests deliberated about whom they should appoint to the position of Zechariah. The lot fell to Simeon. This man, you see, is the one who was informed by the holy spirit that he would not see death until he had laid eyes on the Anointed in the flesh.

◆25◆

NOW I, JAMES, AM THE ONE WHO WROTE this account at the time when an uproar arose in Jerusalem at the death of Herod. I took myself to the wilderness until the uproar in Jerusalem died down. There I praised the Lord God, who gave me the wisdom to write this account.

Grace will be with all those who fear the Lord. Amen.

ABOUT THE TRANSLATION

This translation is part of the Scholars Version translation, published by Polebridge Press. An original translation of all the canonical and non-canonical Gospel
texts, the Scholars Version is the first major new translation of these texts prepared without ecclesiastical or
religious control. The translation offers the modern
reader the opportunity to experience the original vital-
ity and spirit of these texts. The fresh and contemporary
language of these translations is being used by a growing number of writers and scholars.

The Scholars Version translation of the Infancy
Gospel of James appears in *The Infancy Gospel of James
and Thomas*, published by Polebridge Press. As part of

the Scholars Bible series, the book presents the translated Gospel side-by-side with the original language text, along with introduction, notes and glossary.

The Scholars Version translation of all the known Gospels and Gospel fragments from the early Christian era, including the Infancy Gospel of James, appears in *The Complete Gospels*, edited by Robert J. Miller and published by Polebridge Press.

For information about these books and the Scholars Version translations, contact Polebridge Press, P.O. Box 6144, Santa Rosa, CA 95406.

Suggestions for further Reading

Ronald F. Hock, *The Infancy Gospels of James and Thomas*. Scholars Bible 2; Santa Rosa, CA: Polebridge Press, 1995 (contains the Greek text and an English translation of the Infancy Gospel of James).

Jan Gijsel and Rita Beyers, *Libri de Nativitate Mariae*. Corpus Christianorum. Series Apocryphorum 9-10. Brepols: Turnhout, 1997 (contain the Latin texts and French translations of the Gospel of Pseudo-Matthew and The Book of the Birth of Mary).

David R. Cartlidge and J. Keith Elliott, *Art and the Christian Apocrypha*. New York: Routledge, 2001.

Heidi J. Hornik and Mikeal C. Parsons, *Illuminating Luke: The Infancy Narrative in Italian Renaissance Painting*. Harrisburg, PA: Trinity Press International, 2003.

Vasiliki Limberis, Divine Heiress: *The Virgin Mary and the Creation of Christian Constantinople*. New York: Routledge, 1994.

Jaroslav Pelikan, *Mary through the Centuries: Her Place in the History of Culture*. New Haven: Yale University Press, 1996.

Stefano Zuffi, *Gospel Figures in Art*. Trans. T. M. Hartmann; Los Angeles: Jean Paul Getty Museum, 2003.

OTHER ULYSSES/SEASTONE TITLES

The Gospel of Thomas:
Unearthing the Lost Words of Jesus
John Dart & Ray Riegert
Introduction by John Dominic Crossan, $11.95
This accessible translation of The Gospel of Thomas allows
readers to find a Jesus unadulterated by 2000 years of myth and
interpretation—a strikingly different figure from the portrait in
the New Testament.

The Historical Mary:
Revealing the Pagan Identity of the Virgin Mother
Michael Jordan, $14.00
Based on fresh research of ancient Near Eastern, Jewish and
early Christian texts, this book unravels the mystery of who
Mary really was and what role she played in Jesus' life and an-
cient society.

Jesus and Moses: The Parallel Sayings
Joey Green
Introduction by Rabbi Stewart Vogel, $19.00
Jesus and Moses presents the sayings of Jesus and the parallel
teachings of Judaism found in the Old Testament, Talmud and
other Jewish works. Hardback.

The Lost Gospel Q: The Original Sayings of Jesus
Marcus Borg, Editor
Introduction by Thomas Moore, $11.95
The sayings within this book represent the very first Gospel.
Here is the original Sermon on the Mount, the Lord's Prayer
and Beatitudes. Reconstructed by biblical historians, Q provides
a window into the world of ancient Christianity.

The Lost Sutras of Jesus: Unlocking the Ancient Wisdom of the Xian Monks
Edited by Ray Riegert & Thomas Moore, $18.00

Combining the amazing story of the writing of the sutras, their disappearance and rediscovery and an exploration of their message, The Lost Sutras of Jesus is a fascinating historical journey. It is also a unique spiritual quest into the heart of Jesus' teachings and the essence of Eastern religion. Hardback.

Music of Silence:
A Sacred Journey through the Hours of the Day
David Steindl-Rast & Sharon Lebell
Introduction by Kathleen Norris, $12.00

A noted Benedictine monk shows us how to incorporate the sacred meaning of monastic life into our everyday world by paying attention to the "seasons of the day" and the enlivening messages to be found in each moment.

12 Tribes, 10 Plagues & the 2 Men Who Were Moses: A Historical Journey into Biblical Times
Graham Phillips, $14.95

From the Exodus and the ten plagues of Egypt to the conquest of Canaan and the battle between David and Eshbaal at the Pool of Gibeon, this book shows that many fascinating Old Testament stories can in fact be scientifically corroborated.

To order these books call 800-377-2542 or 510-601-8301, fax 510-601-8307, e-mail ulysses@ulyssespress.com, or write to Ulysses Press, P.O. Box 3440, Berkeley, CA 94703. All retail orders are shipped free of charge. California residents must include sales tax. Allow two to three weeks for delivery.